PHILADELPHIA ARCHITECTURE

MW00397586

14⁹⁵

GREEK AND ROMAN COUPLING, THE SECOND BANK OF THE UNITED STATES, C. 1970.
Architect William Strickland deigned this Greek Revival building with plain Doric columns
and little decoration. The Greek brick façade with marble exterior has a Roman interior.
Designed to resemble the Parthenon in Athens, the Second Bank is now the National Portrait
Gallery containing many portraits of the nation's founding fathers. In the 19th century, Charles
Dickens wrote, "It was a handsome building of white marble which had a mournful, ghost-like
aspect dreary to behold. . . . I hastened to inquire its name and purpose, and then my surprise
vanished. It was the tomb of many fortunes, the great catacomb of investment—the memorable
U.S. Bank." (PHC.)

PHILADELPHIA ARCHITECTURE

THOM NICKELS

ARCADIA

Copyright © 2005 by Thom Nickels
ISBN 0-7385-3798-5

Published by Arcadia Publishing
Charleston SC, Chicago IL, Portsmouth NH, San Francisco CA

Printed in the United States of America

Library of Congress Catalog Card Number: 2005920282

For all general information contact Arcadia Publishing at:
Telephone 843-853-2070
Fax 843-853-0044
E-mail sales@arcadiapublishing.com
For customer service and orders:
Toll-Free 1-888-313-2665

Visit us on the Internet at www.arcadiapublishing.com

For my father, Thomas C. Nickels, architect (1925–1986), and grandfather, Frank V. Nickels, architect (1890–1985).

THE OLDEST HOUSE IN PHILADELPHIA, 1994. Philadelphia's oldest house is located on West River Drive. Built by Swedes in 1660, the house is also known as Bollsen Cottage. It was surveyed by Thomas Holme in 1684, although the house was constructed 24 years earlier. (David S. Traub.)

CONTENTS

Acknowledgments   6

Introduction   7

1.   Old Philadelphia   11

2.   Streetscapes and Houses   53

3.   The Modern Houses and Beyond   101

ACKNOWLEDGMENTS

The genesis of this book began, really, with Arcadia editor Erin Loftus's "insistence" that I start another project. Since I come from a family of Philadelphia architects, writing a book on the subject seemed natural. AIA architect David S. Traub, a friend and colleague, offered images from his Philadelphia streetscape collection, books from his Walnut Street office, and tidbits of information and insight. Thanks are extended to the Philadelphia Historical Commission (PHC), especially to Randal Baron, Laura M. Spina, and Jonathan Farnham, Ph.D. Without their patient rummaging through files, I would still be canvassing the town in search of (expensive) images. The firm of Robert Venturi in Manayunk was also responsive; no sooner did I put out a call for submissions than a package arrived at my door. Architect David S. Slovic was also helpful, as were St. Mark's Anglo Catholic Church, Father Shinn of St. Andrew's Russian Orthodox Church, Howard Haas, and photographers Robert Gordon, Joel Kaylor, and Tom Bernard. Rosemarie Fabien, Ph.D., of the Hiller Group Hillier Architects was a major asset, as was much-published Philadelphia photographer Joe Nettis (*Philadelphia Discovered*), now retired, who invited David Traub and me to his studio to search his trove of images and take what we wanted.

Thanks also go to *Metro*, the Philadelphia newspaper that provided me with a forum for architectural writing (the weekly column "Building Blocks"), and to Bob Christian, publisher of Philadelphia's *Weekly Press*.

AN ANGEL IN THE PEN, *C.* **1980.** This painting, done by a prisoner many years ago, was discovered on the walls of one of the solitary confinement cells in Eastern State Penitentiary. Solitary confinement, according to the early Quakers, was the best way to seek divine guidance and forgiveness for criminal activities. (PHC.)

INTRODUCTION

Consider the great event in architecture when the walls parted and columns became.
—Louis I. Kahn

To be in the presence of a great work of architecture is such a satisfaction that you can go hungry for days.
—Philip Johnson

I grew up in a world of drafting boards and blueprints. My grandfather Frank V. Nickels was nearly finished with his architectural career when I came of age. My father, Thomas C., died before his dream of becoming a great architect could be realized. His work included homes, churches, and strip malls on Philadelphia's Main Line, as well as a house-in-the-round in Scarsdale, New York, for NBC sportscaster Joe Garagiola. My grandfather designed a number of city projects, including Philadelphia's Nazareth Hospital and a series of townhouses on Lombard Street, the latter noted in Russell Weigley's book *Philadelphia: A 300-Year History.*

Having an architect for a parent made me appreciate buildings from an early age. From the time I was a toddler, my father would take the family on long country rides in order to show us old stone homes, churches, and various historic sites throughout Chester and Bucks Counties. These jaunts inevitably included the recitation of names like Vincent Kling, Frank Lloyd Wright, and Louis I. Kahn, all famous architects of the period and men I assumed my father wished to emulate.

It was Kling who most fascinated him, perhaps because they were close in age and because he saw something in Kling's work that resembled his own. Often my father would ruminate on the prominence of the Kling partnership in Philadelphia and how difficult it was for other architects to get in on the action. Kling, born and raised in East Orange, New Jersey, was the son of a builder. After a stint in the navy, he worked in New York at the office of Skidmore, Owings, and Merrillas. Soon after he came to Philadelphia, his firm became the city's largest, with over 400 employees.

As principal architect and planner, Kling, along with Philadelphia city planner Edmund Bacon, was responsible for the creation of Penn Center. His handsome red granite 53-story Bell Atlantic Tower was another addition to the city. *New York Times* architecture critic Paul Goldberger compared the Bell Atlantic Tower to 30 Rockefeller Plaza and commented that it was "a fun, stable presence on the skyline, with enough rhythm to its shape to keep the eye engaged."

The creation of Penn Center on the site of the Frank Furness–designed Chinese Wall and the old Pennsylvania Railroad was a monumental step in the shaping of modern Philadelphia. Before Penn Center, much of downtown Philadelphia was a massive enclosure surrounding a labyrinth of train tracks. The Wall resembled an industrial fortress, a Fort Knox of trains and wires, a city within a city. The post-industrial age mandated that this giant Furness creation be replaced.

During his lifetime, Furness's eccentric architectural designs often made him an object of disdain. In the New York atelier of Richard Morris, Furness learned what critics call the "medievalized eclectic forms" that he popularized in Philadelphia. By the 1860s, despite differing opinions about his work, he was one of Philadelphia's highest paid architects. By the end of his life, he had designed nearly 650 buildings in the city. In fact, Furness buildings were once so common that historic preservationists barely noticed when they were torn down to make way for parking lots or garages.

While Penn Center's boxy, flat-top high rises gave new life to the city, some of Edmund Bacon's other projects, like City Hall Plaza, are seen as failures. Architecture critic Inga Saffron noted, "Bacon really is an important historic figure, who dragged an insular, smoke-blackened Philadelphia into the modern age during his 21 years as director of the Philadelphia Planning Commission. . . . For all Bacon did to keep Philadelphia a living city, his dull city hall plazas, blank-walled buildings and highway canyons leave it forever scarred."

Bacon's failed plazas are a minor glitch in his resume when one considers his contribution to the revitalization of Society Hill. An example of this is E. M. Pei's 32-story Society Hill Towers. These buildings could be viewed as precursors to changes in the Philadelphia skyline. Pei, who studied under Walter Gropius at Harvard, made use of pilotis, as well as the glass façade, to create what many have called a masterpiece. Upon their completion in the mid-1960s, Society Hill Towers pointed to the next step in Philadelphia's architectural progression: the breaking of the so-called 100-year "gentleman's agreement" that no high-rise in the city could be taller than the statue of William Penn atop city hall. This stipulation had inspired an almost religious belief that Penn's hat was the city's cosmic ceiling, and that the height limitation had been ordained by providence. So persuasive was the belief at the time that there was even a popular Philadelphia talk show called "Under Billy Penn's Hat."

Quaker influence curtailed ostentatious architectural displays or the urge to create showy masterpieces. John MacArthur's Second Empire city hall was certainly an exception to the rule, enough to make the AIA comment, "William Penn's Quaker sensibilities would have been shaken by the grand scale and ornateness of City Hall and the Broad Street Station."

During the building height controversy, some declared war on Murphy and Jahn Associates's One Liberty Place, a 61-story tower sheathed in a combination of sapphire-blue glass and metal proposed by developer Willard Rouse. Edmund Bacon himself was against the breaking of the height limit, even if astute critics compared Jahn's structure to William Van Alen's Chrysler Building in New York, noting that Liberty Place had a "more robust body" and "used more modern materials" than the Chrysler Building. Rouse's proposal was hotly debated, with architectural reactionaries predicting the "end of a great Philadelphia tradition" and others implying that usurping the beloved hat would help usher in the "death of western civilization."

That debate's fierce velocity was reminiscent of the brouhaha around George Howe and William Lescaze's PSFS building at Twelfth and Market Streets. Banned from the 1932 Architectural League of New York Annual Exhibition, the PSFS building was at first deemed an "ugly and illogical design." Howe then said of the league, "Like all institutions which have become traditional, it tends to resent change." A contentious Elbert Conover commented on the PSFS building for Philadelphia's *T-Square Club Journal* in March 1931, "The day will come when even in America, we will become skillful enough to meet economic pressure without forcing upon the community such ugliness and such illogical designing."

Conover was made to eat his words in 1939, when Howe and Lescaze were awarded the gold medal of the AIA's Philadelphia chapter. In 1969, the PSFS building received the Building of the Century Award from the same organization. Hailed as the first effort to apply the so-called International Style to the American skyscraper, architecture critic Spiro Kostoff added that perhaps the building "was too coolly self-possessed, too intellectual perhaps, to start a trend."

But even these spectacular new skyscrapers were not enough to make Philadelphia lose its link with the past.

That past includes Colonial master builders Robert Smith and Samuel Rhoads, Greek Revivalists William Strickland and Thomas Ustick Walter, as well as Samuel Sloan, Frank Furness, T. P. Chandler Jr., Benjamin Henry Latrobe, John Notman, Horace Trumbauer, and William Johnston (designer of Philadelphia's first skyscraper, the Jayne Building, at 242–244 Chestnut Street). Along with Paul Philippe Cret, Louis I. Kahn (whose Richards Medical Laboratory many consider the best example of contemporary architecture in the city), Elizabeth Fleisher (award-winning designer of the Parkway House and the fourth woman in Pennsylvania's history to become a registered architect), Robert Venturi, and Denise Scott Brown, Philadelphia's blend of old and new is nothing less than a mix of monumental proportions.

One example is an early design by William Strickland.

Nearly hidden behind a grove of trees, Holy Trinity Romanian Orthodox Church on North Bodine Street stands as a living relic of the early 19th century. Built in 1815 as St. John's Episcopal Church, the building was planned as early as 1764 by 17 members of the Coates family who wished to provide a worship venue for those in communion with the Church of England.

The structure was designed by Strickland (1788–1854), one of the most important architects of post-colonial America. An early building from the free neoclassical period, it is also the earliest surviving structure designed by Strickland, the architect of the Merchant's Exchange Building and the United States Capitol. Church records indicate that there are numerous design connections to other prominent architects of the period, namely Philadelphian Benjamin H. Latrobe. One early historian noted, "The church's interior, fairly conventional in arrangement, is almost as boldly characterized as the exterior, with the curves of the loft and galleries answering that of the altar portico, charging the space, and transforming it into something powerful and novel."

Not long after William Penn's surveyor, Thomas Holme, arranged Philadelphia streets in a grid system with public parks or squares in the 1600s, the early colonists began to build rows of narrow, two-story brick houses. In the 1700s, houses for the rich in the Georgian style began to spring up all over the city. Examples of Philadelphia Georgian architecture include Christ Church at Second and Market Streets, and Benjamin Chew's house, Cliveden, in Germantown. Due to Quaker influence, however, the décor on all Colonial buildings of the time was kept simple.

Another notable building, Memorial Hall, constructed for the 1876 centennial, was threatened with the wrecking ball. Philadelphia's *Evening Bulletin* carried the following headline in October 1958: "Park Board Ponders Crumbling Memorial Hall; Should It Be Fixed for $200,000 or Torn Down?" A surveyor's report at the time described leaks in the hall's dome and a ruined interior, the result of a 30-year vacancy. The condition of the statue of Columbia atop the 160-foot dome indicated the extent of the decay: the feminine personification of America had cracked ankles, and leaves were missing from her wreath.

In 1876, Columbia's glory intact, her view of the Centennial Exposition's 195 buildings included dignitaries like Pres. Ulysses S. Grant, the emperor and empress of Brazil, 4,000 militiamen, and 76,000 onlookers, and a symphony playing a special piece, "Centennial," composed by Richard Wagner.

Originally named the Art Gallery, Memorial Hall was the only exposition structure built for permanence. The architect, Philadelphian Herman J. Schwarzmann, volunteered the design after a city-wide contest for the best rendering. Schwarzmann's building later influenced the design of public structures in Europe, as well as the design of government buildings in the three national expositions following the one in Philadelphia.

Memorial Hall hosted thousands of visitors on May 10, 1876, the exposition's opening day. On display were paintings, sculpture, architectural designs, and photographic exhibits from around the world. The *Centennial Year* newspaper described the event as a time when "Egyptians jostled Quakers, and Arabs nudged Mennonites; a thousand dialects made confusion worse confounded."

Renovation work in the 1960s transformed the hall into a setting for banquets and public entertainment. Not since the building housed the Philadelphia Museum of Art (1877–1920s) had there been so much fuss about keeping Columbia's domain intact. The 7,100-square-foot structure, which has been compared to the Reichstag building in Berlin, needed something more than two city offices, a mini-sports complex, and the redemptive "Ahh!" of history to bring it into the modern era.

Enter the 1976 bicentennial and a memo by Mayor Frank Rizzo describing how an eight-tiered, 42-foot America birthday cake would be "carved up and distributed to area institutions, according to its baker, Sara Lee." Rizzo's conversion of Memorial Hall into a "Centennial Museum" combining artifacts and elements from both 1876 and 1976 celebrations met the goal of offering something more than a desk of brochures.

New Philadelphia buildings, especially two Robert A. M. Stern skyscrapers planned for downtown, will continue to change the city's skyline. The unchangeable thing about Philadelphia, however, continues to be its rich streetscapes. As noted Philadelphia architect David S. Traub, a former associate of Louis I. Kahn, wrote, "Philadelphia is distinguished from other large American cities by virtue of its sense of intimacy, density, walk ability and a flavor of antiquity unusual for a North American city. The narrow street symbolizes all of this. These streets are the emotional dimension of our city's design, balancing the rational geometric grid of William Penn's plan."

A LONG AND WINDING ROAD, 1910. The Lit Brothers building was designed by Collins and Autenrieth Architects. Construction began in 1859 and lasted until 1906. The building, which covers an entire city block, was restored and converted into a three-level retail and banking center in the mid-1990s by Vince Hauser Architects. Philadelphian Gersil N. Kay, a member of the AIA Preservation Committee, led a successful effort to save the building. (PHC.)

LIT BROTHERS DEPARTMENT STORE AND GIMBLES, EIGHTH AND MARKET STREETS, C. 1909. The pandemonium of rush hour is seen here after a light snow. (PHC.)

One

OLD PHILADELPHIA

Architecture begins where engineering ends.

—Walter Gropius

TO BE IMPROVED WITH MODERN STORE, 1938. Number 1334–1336 Chestnut Street in downtown Philadelphia is pictured in 1938. (PHC.)

A BUILDING NOT THERE ANYMORE, 1910. The Mint Arcadia building, located on the northwest corner of Chestnut and Juniper Streets, stands beside John Wanamaker's office window (second floor, right). (PHC.)

GREEK REVIVAL, 2005. In 1833, the board of directors of the Philadelphia Merchant's Exchange celebrated the placing of the cap stone atop the first stock exchange in the country. Designed by William Strickland in an elaborate Greek Revival style with a lantern copied from the Choragic Monument of Lysicrates, this building also had mosaic floors, a domed ceiling, and frescoes on the walls. On the day of the dedication in 1833, Strickland toasted the 140 artisans and working men who collaborated on the building, complimenting their "good conduct and orderly deportment," which he saw as being as "remarkable as their skill and excellence of workmanship." (Joel Kaylor.)

EVERY ACTOR OF NOTE, 1900. As the oldest theater in America, the Walnut Street Theater was designed in 1809 by John Haviland, famous for his designs of prisons. Haviland, who was born in England, came to the United States at the urging of John Quincy Adams. Haviland's three volume book *The Builder's Assistant*, explained the five orders of architecture for the use of carpenters, masons, plasterers, and cabinet makers. The Walnut Street Theater has been home to every actor of note during the 19th and 20th centuries. (PHC.)

THE BIRTH OF THE SCALPEL, C. 1920. As the first hospital in the Pennsylvania colonies, Pennsylvania Hospital (built 1755–1794) boasted a circular amphitheater where modern surgery was first performed in the United States. The building was designed by Samuel Rhoads and David Evans Jr. (PHC.)

DO THESE BONES LIVE? WASHINGTON SQUARE, 1910. Breaking ground for the Curtis Center in 1910 meant skirting the perimeter of Washington Square, one of William Penn's five original squares laid out by Penn's surveyor Thomas Holme, in 1682. Originally called Southeast Square, Washington Square was used as a potter's field and mass grave for "strangers in the city." Prior to the Revolution, the square was used as pasture field. In the 1700s, Washington's fallen troops were buried in the square. Bodies were wrapped in canvas and in some instances piled on top of one another in mass graves. In the 1800s, the black community used the square for Mexican Day of the Dead style celebrations. Two creeks flowed through the square at this time. The creeks were filled with two to six inch fish and crayfish. (PHC.)

THE DREAM GARDEN, 1970. Edgar Seeler designed the Curtis Center on the north side of Washington Square in 1910. The Beaux Arts building was home to the *Ladies Home Journal* as well as the Curtis Publishing Company. The Curtis building lobby is home to the Tiffany studios glass mosaic recreation of Maxfield Parish's *The Dream Garden*, a work containing 1,001 pieces of hard-fired glass in 260 color tones. The 15 feet tall by 49 feet wide mural was threatened with removal in 1994 when Las Vegas casino monger Steve Wynn sought to move the work to a casino. Grassroots efforts, especially the work of Arts Defense League, spearheaded a successful city-wide movement against the move. (PHC.)

CHURCH ALONG THE ROAD, C. 1959. Holy Trinity Romanian Orthodox Church stands on North Bodine Street. Built in 1815 as St. John's Episcopal Church, it was leased in 1923 to the Romanians for a mere $15 a year. In 1972, the Episcopal Diocese gave the church to the congregation. Designed by William Strickland (1788–1854), it is his earliest surviving building.

BEAUTIFUL ST. MARK'S CHURCH, C. 1950. Designed by architect John Notman (1810–1865) in the decorated Gothic style of the late 13th and 14th centuries, St. Mark's was built between 1848 and 1849. The church had a plain interior prior to the growth of the Oxford movement within the Catholic wing of the Anglican Church. The Oxford movement stressed ritual, solemnity, and liturgical beauty. St. Mark's rich iconography can be seen in the seven Renaissance-style sanctuary lamps near the high altar; the exquisite pulpit designed by church architect Ralph Adams Cram; and the Lady Chapel, with its silver altar and altarpiece, built as a funeral chapel by Rodman Wanamaker for his deceased wife, Fernanda Henry, in 1900. (St. Mark's Parish.)

A PALACE IN THE PARK, *C.* **1929.** Originally named the Art Gallery, Memorial Hall was the only 1876 Centennial Exposition structure built for permanence. The architect, Herman J. Schwarzmann, volunteered the design after a city-wide contest for the best rendering produced only projects too expensive to actually create. Schwarzmann's building later influenced the design of public buildings in the three national expositions following the one in Philadelphia. At the centennial's opening, the building housed dignitaries like Pres. Ulysses S. Grant and the emperor and empress of Brazil, as well as 76,000 onlookers. Richard Wagner composed the special symphonic piece "Centennial" for the occasion. (PHC.)

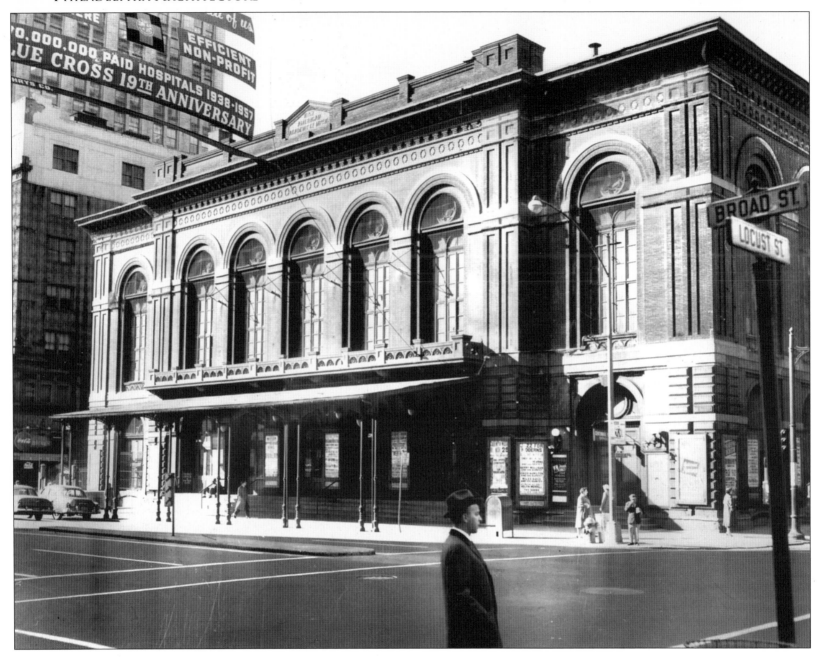

THE QUAKERS WERE WRONG ABOUT ENTERTAINMENT, *C.* 1958. Philadelphia was a Johnny-come-lately to the world of musical development. Quakerism, for all its fine attributes in the fields of peace and justice, tended to downplay entertainment and the arts. In 1855–1857, a design modeled after La Scala in Milan was selected for a site on South Broad Street, now known as the Avenue of the Arts. The lavish neo-Baroque interior is one of the most spectacular in the city. Huge Corinthian columns decorate the proscenium, and a Victorian chandelier illuminates the Karl Heinrich Schmalze–designed murals on the ceiling. (PHC.)

CASTLES IN THE AIR, *C.* **1873.** Soaring like a Norman cathedral, the Masonic temple at 1 North Broad Street was designed by architect James Windrim and took five years to build. By its completion in 1873, the total cost of construction had reached $1.6 million. The temple's elaborate halls were decorated over a span of 20 years. With names like Egyptian Hall, Norman Hall, and Renaissance Hall, the temple rivals the ornamentation of the city's great cathedrals. On the grand staircase are hand-carved sculptures by William Rush, and in the temple's museum and library, one can see George Washington's Masonic apron, a fabric embroidered by the wife of the Marquis de Lafayette. (PHC.)

THE CENTER OF HUMAN CONCOURSE, C. 1875. The debate as to where to build city hall began in 1838. Many wanted city hall to be built on Independence Square, the site of Independence Hall. Fortunately the state legislature nixed the idea so a referendum was held, and Philadelphians selected Penn Square. The cornerstone was laid on July 4, 1874. Pictured are the eight-foot thick slabs of concrete used for the building's foundation. (PHC.)

IN THE NAVY, 1975. The William Strickland designed Naval Home on Grays Ferry Avenue was planned in 1826 and built *c.* 1830. The building was used as a Naval home and hospital until 1846. It was also the nation's first Naval academy. The British occupied the building during the Revolution, when it served as headquarters to Gen. Pattison, commander of the royal artillery. In 1976 the home closed when the Naval Hospital moved to Mississippi. Today it is a 20-acre gated condo and townhouse community. (PHC.)

NAVAL HOME, 1838. This lithograph of the Naval Home was created by J. C. Wild ©
1804–1846).

FURNESS THE OBSCURE, C. 1965. The Pennsylvania Academy of the Fine Arts was designed in 1871 and completed in 1876. It was Furness's first project of national significance. In *The Architecture of Frank Furness*, James F. O'Gorman wrote, "Frank Furness lived until 1912; several of his last years were spent in ill health. They must not have been happy ones, and his reputation as a disagreeable person was accordingly enhanced. He died in near obscurity, amid his flowers and horses at 'Idlewild.' The local papers barely mentioned that he had been an architect and thus began a neglect that was to last for half a century." (PHC.)

PENNSYLVANIA ACADEMY OF THE FINE ARTS EXTERIOR. As the nation's oldest art school and museum, the interior of the Pennsylvania Academy of the Fine Arts is rich with hues of blue, yellow, and red. The grand staircase also adds an element of grandeur. The academy's fine collection include works by Benjamin West, Winslow Homer, Thomas Eakins, Andrew Wyeth, Red Grooms, and Charles Wilson Peale. (PHC.)

ALL ROADS LEAD TO ART, C. 1930. Architect Horace Trumbauer designed the Philadelphia Museum of Art. Construction by the commissioners of Fairmount Park began in 1919 through funds provided by the city. Built on the site of an old reservoir, the structure's neoclassical design reflected the Roman temple neoclassicism of the waterworks. Made of pure Minnesota dolomite (kasota stone), with glazed blue roof tiles meshed with Polychrome finials and pediments, the building suffered during the Depression. Thanks to the Works Progress Administration and grants, the interior construction of galleries was resumed. While museum director Fiske Kimball (1888–1955) is credited with making the museum one of the nation's best, president J. Stogdell Stokes, serving from 1933 to 1947, is credited with revitalizing the museum during the Depression. (PHC.)

UNITS OF THREE, C. 1972. The First Unitarian Church of Philadelphia was completed in 1885. Designed by Frank Furness, it actually replaced an earlier Unitarian church on another site by William Strickland. Strickland's church had replaced Robert Mills's octagonal church of 1812. (PHC.)

OLD ORIGINAL WANAMAKER'S, *C.* **1900.** The original Wanamaker's building is seen here prior to the construction of the new store by Chicago architect Daniel Burnham. (PHC.)

INDEPENDENCE HALL, 2005. Designed by Alexander Hamilton and Edmund Wooley, Independence Hall is an excellent example of Georgian style. Once known as the State House, in 1729 it became the seat of government after lawmakers transferred the site from town hall at Second and Market Streets. In 1750, the Assembly voted to add a tower to the rear of the State House. From 1790 to 1800, the State House served as the U.S. Capitol before its move to Washington. John Haviland was hired by the city to renovate the building in 1830. (David S. Traub.)

PHILADELPHIA CITY HALL, C. 1980.
Construction on city hall began in
1871 after a year of planning. Scottish
architect John McArthur Jr. was selected
to design the building, and work was
completed 30 years later, in 1901. The
Palais des Tuileries and the new Louvre
in Paris influenced the building's design.
In 1873, Alexander Milne Calder started
the sculpture work; at the same time,
construction on the tower commenced.
The High Victorian Picturesque or
French Renaissance building had
many starts and stops, as funding was
a common problem. After McArthur's
death in 1890, John Ord was appointed
the new architect. Ord resigned in 1893
over a wage dispute and was replaced
by W. Bleddyn Powell. The structure
now contains a turreted courtyard stair
tower, a slate mansard roof with dormer
windows, and paired columns. The tower
reaches a height of 337 feet, the tallest
masonry tower in the world. A series
of synchronized lights were installed in
the tower to regulate traffic along Broad
Street. The experiment pleased some, but
many could not see the lights, suffering
craned necks and an early version of road
rage. (PHC.)

THE CURTIS INSTITUTE OF MUSIC, 1980. Architects Brack and Douglas Gordon designed the Curtis Institute of Music on Rittenhouse Square in 1897. Once the home of banker George Childs Drexel, the building was used as an all-scholarship music school in 1924 after its founding by Mary Louise Curtis Bok Zimbalist. Famous composers and musicians who taught and studied here include Samuel Barber, Gian Carlo Menotti, Leonard Bernstein, Anna Moffo, and Ned Rorem. (PHC.)

READING TERMINAL, C. 1920S. Designed by Francis Harry Kimball in 1891, the Reading Terminal has been likened to "a wide level cliff with a cave at its base." At one point, 45,000 people passed through the terminal every day. The food market beneath the train shed sold delicacies from around the world. In the 1980s, the train shed was transformed into the $600 million new Philadelphia Convention Center. The Reading Terminal Market still prospers and has become famous in the city for its diverse foods. (PHC.)

STONE WALLS FOR A PRISON, C. 1974. Sometimes called "the single most historic building in Philadelphia," Eastern State Penitentiary was designed by John Haviland in 1820 and 1821. Haviland's plan—seven corridors radiating out from a central rotunda—was adopted by architects around the world for other penitentiaries. When Charles Dickens visited the site in 1842, he reported that a prisoner grabbed his coat and wept. "I never saw or heard any kind of misery that impressed me more than the wretchedness of this man," he wrote. In 1988, Mayor W. Wilson Goode stated, "This historical site must be preserved." (PHC.)

ACADEMY OF MUSIC EXTERIOR, 1924. On the Academy of Music's stage, Dom Pedro, emperor of Brazil, spoke during the centennial. The greatest orators of the day—Henry Clay, Daniel Webster, William Lloyd Garrison, Henry Ward Beecher—also spoke there. (PHC.)

FRANK LLOYD WRIGHT SOAPBOX, 1968. Just off Rittenhouse Square, on South Eighteenth Street, stands the Art Alliance, formerly the Wetherill Mansion. Designed by Charles Klauder of Frank Miles Day and Brothers Architects in 1936, the Art Alliance hosted exhibits and lectures by Le Corbusier and Frank Lloyd Wright. In 1952, the works of Bauhaus architect Walter Gropius were displayed. Writer Anais Nin also lectured here in the 1970s. (PHC.)

AN UNCOMPROMISING MASTERPIECE, 1975. Critics sum up Frank Furness's library at the University of Pennsylvania as "an uncompromising masterpiece." Opened in 1891, the Victorian Gothic building is a combination of materials of varied colors and textures. Despite its terra cotta ornament, its Palladian window, and a design reminiscent of a Romanesque church, the Furness library fell into obscurity. James F. O'Gorman attributes the decline to McKim, Mead, and White's design of the Boston Public Library. He states, "Stylistically McKim's work was to dominate the immediate future. . . . McKim prepared the way for the disciplined architectural style that was to bury Furness' work in obscurity for the next 50 years." (PHC.)

DEATH HAS ITS PRIVILEGES, C. 1957. The Athenaeum of Philadelphia, founded in 1814, is a private subscription library supported by members. The building was designed by John Notman in the Italian Revival style and built in 1845. The interior is decorated with early-19th-century American furniture and fine arts. During construction, the foundation of the Walnut Street prison was discovered beneath the site. The Athenaeum houses 180,000 architectural drawings, 350,000 photographs, and manuscripts representing the work of 1,000 American architects. William Strickland was the first architect in Philadelphia to become a member. In 1961, Alfred Bendiner wrote in *Bendiner's Philadelphia*, that to become a member of the Athenaeum "you have to wait for another old Philadelphian to die and have his family relinquish the share, so it's available to some other old Philadelphian." Next to the Athenaeum, mayor Richardson Dilworth's house is under construction. (PHC.)

IF I HAD A HAMMER, C. 1920. The Carpenters' Company was founded in 1724 as an organization dedicated to assisting contractors and clients in the building trades. Robert Smith's design shows a cruciform plan based on one of Palladio's Italian villas. Smith also had one of the town halls in his native Scotland in mind when he designed the building. The First Continental Congress was held in Carpenters' Hall and was attended by George Washington as a Virginia delegate, as noted in his diary entries for September 6 to October 17, 1774. (PHC.)

THE RODIN IN WINTER, 1963. Jacques Greber and Paul Cret, the designers of the Benjamin Franklin Parkway and the Benjamin Franklin Bridge, also designed the Rodin Museum. The building was given to the city by Jules Mastbaum, Philadelphia's famous theatrical magnate. It is home to the artist's most famous works, including busts and figures of Balzac, Gustav Mahler, G. B. Shaw, Victor Hugo, and Pope Benedict XV. (PHC.)

VICTORY OVER WHAT? 2002. The Victory Building, along with Philadelphia City Hall, has been called one of the city's best examples of the Second Empire style. Designed by architect Henry Fernbach as a three-story structure, in the 1890s the building was expanded to six stories by Philip Roos, who raised the original mansard roof. It was added to the National Register of Historic Places in 1980, but a fire in 1983 left the structure vacant for years. According to a Preservation Pennsylvania report in 1993, thousands of dollars were spent for an interior sealing procedure to thwart further decomposition and decay. (PHC.)

THE RED CARPET, C. 1910. The 987-room Bellevue Strafford Hotel was designed by G. W. and W. D. Hewitt and built in 1902–1904. The building was rehabilitated and partially restored in 1978–1979 by Day and Zimmermann. Unfortunately, the hotel's Beaux Arts awnings are gone, replaced by 1950s Bauhausian stainless-steel shields. When the building was completed, it was the most sumptuous hotel in the country, with electric lights installed by Thomas Edison. The Bellevue's sister hotel, also designed by the Hewitts, was New York's original Waldorf Astoria. It was demolished to make way for the Empire State Building. Bram Stoker wrote *Dracula* while a guest at the Bellevue. (Charles Cushing.)

TAILS AND TOP HATS AT THE UNION LEAGUE, C. 1960. Designed by architect John Fraser, the Second Empire–style Union League on Broad Street was one of the few buildings built in Philadelphia during the Civil War. (Tom Bernard.)

TRIBUTE TO JULIAN ABELE, 1980. Architect Horace Trumbauer and his assistant, Julian Abele, designed the Free Library of Philadelphia. Abele, a student of design at the Pennsylvania of the Fine Arts, based his plans on French architect Ange-Jacques Gabriel's twin façades for the Ministry of the Marine and Hotel de la Crillon on the Place de la Concorde in Paris. An African American, Abele received little recognition in his lifetime. The Free Library's existence can be attributed to Dr. William Pepper, who led efforts to found a free library for the public and end the subscription-only system that kept books from the people. (PHC.)

WHITE MARBLE GOTHIC REVIVAL, 1960. Arch Street Methodist Church, a prime example of Gothic Revival architecture, was designed by Addison Hutton (1834–1916). Hutton came to Philadelphia in 1857 and worked as a carpenter and schoolteacher before learning architectural drafting from Samuel Sloan. He spent 40 years of his 53-year career working alone and retired in 1907. (PHC.)

THE LONG-GONE LINCOLN, 1916. A number of architects, including William H. Decker, William Getti, Willis Gaylord, Hale and Thomas, and Preston Lonsdale, worked on the Lincoln Building, also known as the Betz Building, a bank and office complex at 100 South Broad Street. The Lincoln became the future site of the Philadelphia National Bank Building when it was demolished. (PHC.)

THE SPOT WHERE BEN FRANKLIN FLEW HIS KITE, 1957. St. Stephen's Episcopal Church, designed by William Strickland and built in 1822–1823 with a later addition by Frank Furness, began a Gothic revival in church architecture. St. Stephen's is a repository for the country's first stained-glass windows, as well as the largest collection of ecclesiastical work by Tiffany Studios anywhere in the world. (PHC.)

CITY OF THE DEAD, 1970. Laurel Hill Cemetery is spread out over 75 acres and contains more than 33,000 monuments. Referred to as a necropolis, or city of the dead, the cemetery's soaring great obelisks and massive mausoleums overlook Kelly Drive and the Schuylkill River. Laid out by architect John Notman, Laurel Hill became the "afterlife address of choice" in 1836. Here is the funerary art and history at its most Gothic and compelling. Among those interred are Frank Furness, Frederich Groff (Fairmount Water Works), and Maj. Gen. George E. Meade, a Union hero at the Battle of Gettysburg. (PHC.)

JUDGE AND JURY, *C.* **1960.** The tomb of American historian Henry Charles Lea is located at Laurel Hill Cemetery. (PHC.)

DEATH BE NOT PROUD, C. 1969.
Architect Robert Smith designed St. Peter's Anglican Church after neighboring Christ Church became overcrowded. Once called "the Chapel of Ease," this scaled-down Palladian church utilizes round arch windows and a simple design, reflecting early Quaker influences. William Strickland added the steeple in 1852. Built on land donated by Thomas and Rachel Penn, the church cemetery contains the graves of those who embodied the American spirit. (PHC.)

ST. PETER'S CHURCH, C. 1950. As the Philadelphia Foundation for Architecture noted in 1994, St. Peter's Church still retains its original high-backed pews, all raised above the floor to prevent drafts. (PHC.)

THE ROMAN SPRING OF BENJAMIN LATROBE, C. 2002. Benjamin Latrobe designed Philadelphia's first waterworks in the 1790s as a response to the yellow fever epidemic that wiped out almost 60 percent of Philadelphia's population in one year. Compelled to develop a source of clean water for drinking and sewage, the city established the first waterworks in Center Square. Another site, designed in 1812–1815 by Groff, a draftsman on the original project, was modeled after Roman temples and built on the banks of the Schuylkill River. Lush grounds surrounded the complex, creating a setting that made the waterworks the most popular tourist destination in the United States in the 18th century, after Niagara Falls. (David S. Traub.)

BLOOD IN THE NORTHWEST PARLOR, GRUMBLETHORPE, 1963. John Wister built Grumblethorpe as a county seat in 1744. Wister, who emigrated from Hillspach, Germany, in 1727, quickly became a successful merchant in Philadelphia. Grumblethorpe was built from local stone and timber. Noted as a charitable man, Wister made sure that the bread baked every Saturday was distributed among the poor. During the Battle of Germantown, Gen. James Agnew was wounded and died in the parlor of this house. For many years, blood could still be seen on the floor of the northwest parlor. (PHC.)

FURNESS IN FISHTOWN, 1961. Lower Kensington, a suburb of Philadelphia in the 1700s, is known today as Fishtown, for the ships that used to dispatch their catch on the nearby Delaware River docks. The Furness Building, at Thirty-second and Market Streets, bears a slight resemblance to this building, located at 28 West Girard Avenue. Both have façades that "greet" oncoming traffic from more rural or remote areas. (PHC.)

TRIPLE ONION CROWN, C. 1987. St. Andrew's Russian Orthodox Church, at 705 North Fifth Street, was founded in 1897 and consecrated by Bishop Tikhon, the future patriarch of Moscow, in 1902. Designed by American architect Clyde Smith Adams, the finished church succeeded in merging Russian forms and materials with the neighborhood of Northern Liberties. As the oldest Orthodox church in Philadelphia, both its consecrating bishop and its first priest to celebrate divine liturgy were canonized saints by the Russian Church. The structure's massive purple onion domes leave passers-by awestruck. (Father Mark Shinn.)

Two

STREETSCAPES AND HOUSES

A house is a machine for living in.

—Le Corbusier

POISED LIKE BUSTER KEATON, 1912. This image depicts 2100 Pine Street on a spring day in 1912. Slightly east of the Fitler Square area, this neighborhood includes a number of historical residences, including the homes of naturalist Edward Drinker Cope, the Rosenbach brothers, and war novelist Richard Harding Davis. Civil War general George Meade lived at Nineteenth and Delancey Streets. (PHC.)

ON A SMALL URBAN SITE (THE GUILD HOUSE), 1966. "Inexpensive red clay brick matches an adjacent warehouse, but the brick nearest the sidewalk is of a different size from that where the façade meets the street. The dark walls with double-hung windows recall traditional city row houses, but the effect of the windows is uncommon due to their subtle, unusually big proportions. The scale of the windows also differs according to their distance from the street." (VSBA.)

25 HIGH ST.

SETTLEMENT OF GERMANTOWN, 1957. Germantown was founded in 1683 when a group of Quaker families from Krefeld, Germany, wanted to participate in William Penn's "holy experiment." Francis David Pastorius, a wealthy, aristocratic German intellectual, joined the Krefelders and helped cultivate the area. Pastorius negotiated the purchase of a 5,700-acre tract of land through William Penn, calling it "the German township." Pastorius had one of the largest libraries in the Colonial era. (PHC.)

CLIVEDEN, 6401 GERMANTOWN AVENUE, C. 1950. Prominent Philadelphian Benjamin Chew built Cliveden from 1763 to 1767. The British once occupied this beautiful example of Georgian architecture for six months in 1778. American troops, under Col. Musgrave, attempted to reclaim the house but suffered defeat. Musket burns from that battle can still be seen on the floor of the entrance way. The interior of Cliveden contains Waterford oil lamps and looking glasses used at the fabled Meschianza Ball that Tory Philadelphians gave in honor of British general Sir William Howe. (PHC.)

CLIVEDEN INTERIOR, 1970. According to Alfred Bendiner, "About 1864, Germantown Avenue was Main Street and there was . . . sleigh rides to Valley Green, Indian Head Rock and the beautiful monument to Pastorius in Vernon Park. Hurdy gurdies and hokey pokeys. The mess house and Cliveden. . . . John Harbeson and his chess collection and the Society of the Jolly Grapefruit, Sunday afternoons at the Campbell's playing croquet. Trolley cars, starched, white, long dresses and hair ribbons, ice cream pants and boater straws." (PHC.)

PLEASING MOUNT PLEASANT, C. 1965. The epitome of elegance in Colonial Philadelphia, Mount Pleasant was built by Capt. John McPherson in 1761. Located in the city's 4,000-acre Fairmount Park section, Mount Pleasant included Palladian windows on its east and west sides and corner quoins with a warm-colored stucco ruled to look like stone. (PHC.)

IVY AND THE GILDED AGE, 1973. Frank Furness supervised the construction of the William Rhawn mansion, at 1800 Verree Road in the Fox Chase section of Northeast Philadelphia. Built on 13 acres in what was once considered country, Rhawn named his estate Knowlton after his wife's great-grandfather John Knowles. With its gabled roofs, dormer windows, and expansive porches, Knowlton had all the advanced technologies of the day, such as indoor plumbing and heating. (PHC.)

FRANK FURNESS GETS HIS FEET WET, C. 1980. As one of the first projects designed by the young Frank Furness, the Thomas Hockley House contains the classic Victorian forms, including mansard roof, pointed dormers, and projecting bay windows. Furness's use of brick—the rich textures and patterns—would influence the design of many other houses of the era. (PHC.)

ELFRETH'S ALLEY BEFORE RENOVATION, 1938. Constructed between 1702 and 1704, Elfreth's Alley is the oldest continuous residential street in the country. The street is lined with 32 sixteen-foot-wide Federal and Colonial homes. (PHC.)

COLONEL FREEWAY, 1976. Known as the oldest street in America, Elfreth's Alley predates William Penn's horizontal and perpendicular design of the city. "The architecture has the character of an English village (except small paned double-hung windows instead of casements), paneled shutters and slat shutters, uncarved cornices and wood dormers, paneled front doors with brass knockers," wrote Alfred Bendiner in *Bendiner's Philadelphia*. (PHC.)

DOWN AND OUT IN PHILADELPHIA AND CAMDEN, C. 1986. Not every building and streetscape in Philadelphia is beautifully historical or memorable, yet this old cobblestone back alley, with its two-story houses, could probably tell a historical tale or two. (David S. Traub.)

MURALS AS POWERFUL TOOLS, 2003. A mural transforms this house on Philadelphia's Pine Street. Founded in 1984 under mayor Wilson Goode, the Mural Arts Program began as the Anti-Graffiti Network. Since 1984, Jane Golden has overseen the completion of almost 3,000 indoor and outdoor murals in the city. "Murals are wonderful because they make art accessible to everyone," Golden said. Philadelphia has more public mural projects than any other city in the nation. (David S. Traub.)

ROW HOUSE UPON ROW HOUSE, 1959. In the early 20th century, Kensington was one of the most important iron and steel manufacturing districts in the country. Before that, the inhabitants were fishermen. As an industrial center, Kensington was home to mills, factories, breweries, and machine shops. For decades, the area was the first stop for many immigrants. (Joe Nettis.)

COZY ON VAN PELT STREET, 1996. Van Pelt Street evokes the charm and gothic feel of *Grimm's Fairy Tales*. (David S. Traub.)

THE PHILADELPHIA STORY, 1961. Many of Philadelphia's Main Line mansions were built in the post–Civil War years of the 1870s to the 1920s. A good number of mansions were torn down in the early 1900s. The Depression and the World War II housing boom also caused many estates to be altered into housing developments. Though many mansions were lost, some managed to survive. The upscale gatherings and aristocratic living among wealthy Philadelphians is best exemplified in the film *The Philadelphia Story*, which profiled city socialite Hope Montgomery Scott. (Joe Nettis.)

THE OPEN ARCH, 1980. This miniature majestic archway near Third and Market Streets seems to pull the passer-by inside. (David S. Traub.)

FULL OF ENGLISH CHARM, 2005. People rarely equate Philadelphia's great northeast with shining examples of memorable architecture, but travel to a town known as Bustleton (1946 Welsh Road) and you will think you slipped back in time to a little English village outside London. The main building, the Memorial Church of St. Luke the Beloved Physician, is a blue stone building trimmed with brown stone and bricks. Designed by Richard Upjohn, architect of Manhattan's Trinity Church, St. Luke's interior is a prime example of Upjohn's purity of style. (David S. Traub.)

CONFLUENCE OF STYLES, 2005. It has been said that in Philadelphia, each street leads to smaller and smaller streets and that the alleyways hide small kingdoms of houses. Architectural surprises also await the casual walker. Here, a blend of old and new accents a cobblestone street. (Joel Kaylor.)

DO YOU REMEMBER THE SWEET GREY HOUSE ON THE CORNER?, 1980. Seen here is one of the many handsome Victorian cottages on Conshohocken State Road in Philadelphia's Main Line region. (David S. Traub.)

THE WHITE PARTY, 1980. The so-called bandbox houses on Ringold Street call to mind the purity of milk. (David S. Traub.)

THE LATIMER HOUSE, C. 1995.
According to David Slovic Associates
Architecture and Urban Design,
"In the formal, historical context
of Philadelphia, the Latimer House
respects the urban scale of the street,
but challenges the idea of urban
domestic space. In defiance of the
typical plan of American urban houses,
organized in connected rectangular
spaces receiving minimal front, back
and lateral light, this design makes the
interior courtyard a major connector
of light and space. Contrasting with
the city's typical long and narrow,
brick row houses, the exterior
abandons height for horizontality.
Shaped around the geometry of the
courtyard and the path of light, the
house is an experiment in form, mass,
and proportion. It brings together,
in a subtle, persuasive manner, the
expression of the European courtyard
house, the American industrial loft and
a modern clarity of space, light and
materials." (Catherine Tightz Bogert.)

LATIMER HOUSE STAIRCASE, C. 1995.
Of the house, David Slovic Associates
Architecture and Urban Design stated,
"The concept, organization, forms,
materials and details challenge the
typical urban house. It offers privacy,
light, generosity of space and a direct
connection to the outdoors, generally
found only outside of the city. The
interior open space is carved to gather
sunlight and to expand each vista. House
functions buffer the living space from the
street noise and open to the courtyard."
(Catherine Tightz Bogert.)

LOOKING BACK IN MADISON SQUARE, 1980. South Philadelphia's stunning Madison Square was placed on the Register of Historic Places in 1971. (David S. Traub.)

ELECTRICAL ETERNITY, 1959. In Manayunk, many cemeteries have an Old World flavor, especially St. David's Episcopal churchyard, built in 1833, (not pictured) where, sadly, many tombstones were removed due to vandalism and age. The 1832 St. John the Baptist churchyard (Irish Roman Catholic), and the 1850 St. Mary Assumption's cemetery (German Roman Catholic) also bespeak an earlier era. (Joe Nettis.)

COBBLESTONES, 1980. Women in heels should walk, not run, on Philadelphia's remaining cobblestone streets. (David S. Traub.)

THE LION FOR REAL, 2005. Unlike Logan Square, which was once used as an execution and burial site, Rittenhouse Square, formerly Southwest Square, was once surrounded by brickyards. In 1825, it was renamed in honor of David Rittenhouse, a Philadelphia astronomer and Revolutionary War leader. The 1859 residential building boom resulted in the square becoming the city's most fashionable address. Unfortunately, the mansions that once lined the square gave way to apartment buildings. Paul Cret designed Rittenhouse Square's present layout in 1913. His plan included an oval plaza in the center with walkways from the street arranged on a diagonal, as well as a reflecting pool surrounded by a balustrade. Here, in Central Plaza, is the *Lion Crushing a Serpent* sculpture by French Romantic artist Antoine-Louis Barye. (David S. Traub.)

STONE TRIM DESIGNS, 1980. The homes of Delancey Street are varied and intricate. Second Empire Victorian townhouses with stone trim designs were popular in the late 1880s. One can also spot classical Revival houses that follow the Federalist style. Architect George Howe raised eyebrows when he converted an 1870s townhouse façade into a 1930s masterpiece. He transformed the red brick façade to gray and pale blue (not pictured), a radical departure for the area. (David S. Traub.)

WHERE ARISTOCRATS DINE, C. 2004.
The Cadwalader mansion was built at 2102 Spruce Street during the Civil War antebellum period. The Cadwalader family, one of Philadelphia's most aristocratic, occupied the house from the Civil War until renting it to the French consulate sometime before 1968. The Philadelphia Cadwaladers date from the Revolutionary War, when Charles Wilson Peale painted a series of family portraits. Charles McManus bought the house in 1968. He says, "When I had the house I was able to get all the original lighting fixtures back in the house; there are very few of them left. I even had some of the original mirrors. When I had the house, the rooms were all different colors in the tradition of the period; the halls were ivory and the rugs a crimson red." The Cadwalader house has been featured in the *New York Times*. When the French consulate moved from the building, they took everything, "even the toilet paper," according to McManus. (Joel Kaylor.)

SOUTH PHILADELPHIA WINDOW, 1981. Unarguably one of the oldest ethnically and racially mixed neighborhoods in the nation, South Philadelphia was once home to Thomas Jefferson, who lived here in 1793. (David S. Traub.)

STALKING THE RAVEN, 1960. Born in Boston in 1809, Edgar Allen Poe moved to New York and then Philadelphia after the death of his mother. As the only surviving Poe home in the country, this Philadelphia residence was where Poe wrote "Murder in the Rue Morgue," "The Fall of the House of Usher," as well as a number of other stories and poems. The author's six years in Philadelphia were said to be the most productive and happiest of his life. (Joe Nettis.)

THE MONEY SHOT, 1979. A man takes a leisurely walk along St. Alban's Place. (David S. Traub.)

MANAYUNK HOUSES, 1960. Manayunk's story is really a triumph of the will. Before the Depression, there appeared to be no end to the town's prosperity. In 1909, for instance, people from Philadelphia's Main Line flocked to Manayunk's Main Street to visit the Farmer's Market or the shops open until midnight on a street already crowded with circus-style snake oil salesmen and other amusing hucksters of early-20th-century American life. Even today, Central Philadelphia might be hard-pressed to match the activity that this "sleepless" small town exhibited so many years ago. (Joe Nettis.)

GENTLY DOWN THE STREAM, C. 1999. The Hillier Group relates the following: "Philadelphia is commonly associated with the Liberty Bell or events such as the signing of the Declaration of Independence. But in addition to these benchmarks, there is another side to Philadelphia that might not be as widely known. Unlike the hubbub of the busy city streets, there is also a more serene habitat along the Schuylkill River. During the period between the Civil War and World War II, 11 boathouses were built along the northern bank, creating an area that has come to be known as 'Boathouse Row.'" (Tom Crane.)

FURNESS ON THE WATER, C. 1999. Dating back to May 9, 1856, the barge club was originally organized by 12 Philadelphians, who named the club after a mythological female water spirit from the Legend of Udine. "Originally, the boathouse was only a 50-foot-long x 8-foot wide shed, which cost $100 to build. A little more than 30 years later, the Undine Club commissioned architect Frank Furness to design a permanent stone boathouse at a price of $14,000. The first piles for the boathouse were driven on April 3, 1882," as stated by the Hillier Group. (Tom Crane.)

CENTER CITY ROOFTOPS, 1979. In *Philadelphia Discovered*, Nathaniel Burt wrote the following: "Philadelphia is also a 'City of Homes.' Philadelphia's architecture, as well as its city plan, seems to have been created by Quakers. Whereas New Englanders easily adopted the free-standing frame house, usually white-painted, Philadelphians took to low brick houses flush to the street and connected to each other, a plan of building derived from the English towns from which the first Quaker immigrants came. Even in small Pennsylvania villages this pattern persisted, and in the 19th century developed, after the model of London, into the brick row house, curse or blessing of the city, depending on how well the houses are built." (David S. Traub.)

A NORTHERN LIBERTIES BUNGALOW, 1981. Shown here is one of many unique row houses of Northern Liberties. (David S. Traub.)

THE DENSITY OF IVY, 1981. This gem of a house stands on Philadelphia's Latimer Street. (David S. Traub.)

PORTRAIT OF THE ARTIST, 1979. In the last days of fall, with stacked firewood by the door, a Philadelphian ruminates in his pristine "miles away from the city" urban backyard. (David S. Traub.)

OVER THE RAINBOW, *C.* **2003.** The Olivit-Covenant Presbyterian Church, at Twenty-second and Mount Vernon Streets, is another addition to Philadelphia's rich religious heritage. (Hugh Dillon.)

BEEHIVE PANDEMONIUM, 1962. The Benjamin Franklin Parkway has been called a "cultural Mecca and a triumph of urban planning." This parkway Bauhausian apartment building is one of several high-rise buildings that complement the more classical edifices such as the Free Library, the Rodin Museum, and the Philadelphia Museum of Art. (Joe Nettis.)

BENJAMIN FRANKLIN WAS FRAMED, C. 2000. In a radical departure from conventional museum designs, VSBA reconstructed an astral frame of Benjamin Franklin's house just off Market Street, in Philadelphia's Old City. The steel "ghost" house models the original house that once stood on this site, while the main museum area remains underground. By conserving aboveground space, the site of Franklin's garden is preserved; a few archeological remains of his original house can also be viewed. An astonishing addition is quotes from Franklin's letters to his wife, which are engraved in the paving. Franklin Court is the winner of six prestigious national awards, including the 1984 Presidential Design Award. (VSBA.)

ON A FISHTOWN STREET, C. 1981. Now considered one of the fastest-growing gentrified neighborhoods in the city, Fishtown used to be the laughing stock of real estate snobs. People referred to its inhabitants as "indigenous" or as "toothless yahoos." That concept has changed with time, as well as skyrocketing property values as city dwellers seek new neighborhoods to settle and beautify. (David S. Traub.)

THE GRASS IS GREENER, C. 1981. These Philadelphia houses are located not far from the city's bustling downtown. (David S. Traub.)

THE ANNA VENTURI HOUSE, CHESTNUT HILL, 1992. A seminal work that has influenced architects worldwide, the Anna Venturi house was a recipient of the AIA 25-Year Award in 1989. This little house is everything: closed and open, big and small. Complexity in small-scale buildings creates a hyper busyness—whereas big scale in this small building achieves an appropriate architectural tension, according to VSBA. Called the most significant house of the latter part of the 20th century, it boasts a purposeful ambiguity of design. (Venturi-Scott Brown and Associates.)

HELL'S HIGHWAY (REFORMED), 1979. Camac Street began as a quaint thoroughfare filled with charming houses and tiny gardens. A 1937 pamphlet published by the William Penn Association stated that "Camac Street [had] degenerated into one of the meanest and most notorious streets in the city." Nicknamed "Hell's Highway," the street was the "scene of brawls by day and crimes by night, requiring at times an entire squad of the city's police to maintain order. For 20 years the street, lined with brothels and taverns, rotted in a mire of debauchery. Unkempt derelicts of every sort frequented its dark corners and hideaways." Today, Camac Street is home to some of Philadelphia's best restaurants. Philadelphia Sketch Club—America's oldest continuing artist organization—is also located here. (David S. Traub.)

ANT FARM, c. 1989. South Street's eclectic buildings include everything from the whimsical to the absurd. As the urban boardwalk for the teenage and collegiate quasi-bohemian crowd, South Street has great restaurants and enough ruckus and mayhem to keep you either annoyed or interested. (David S. Traub.)

THE BOYD AND SAM ERIC THEATER, C. 1930. Philadelphia's only art deco movie palace, the Boyd opened in 1928 in a flurry of razzle-dazzle. Designed by architects Hoggman and Henon, the theater was a marvel of handsome lobbies and foyers, French etched glass on lobby mirrors, and a large mural of Greek Amazons near the stage. The 2,500-seat theater stands on the site of the old Aldine Hotel; before the Aldine, the site housed the society mansion of a descendant of Dr. Benjamin Rush. At night, 20 floodlights illuminated the Boyd's marquee. Inside, theatergoers enjoyed the 50-by-30-foot proscenium and the on-stage orchestra pit and organ, which could be raised or lowered mechanically. After the demise of Cinerama in the late 1950s, the Boyd was divided into three smaller theaters. The building was eventually left to decay until a city-wide effort was organized to save it. (Friends of the Boyd.)

THE HILLS ARE ALIVE, C. 1988. Philadelphia's flat but otherwise easy-to-navigate topography puts Manayunk in a class by itself. The hills come as a surprise to first-time visitors, as does the Old World look of the canal. Other Philadelphia neighborhoods may boast of European "connections," but none—except Northern Liberties, with its Eastern Orthodox and Byzantine Catholic Church spires—is as interesting visually. (David S. Traub.)

PHILADELPHIA'S MOST ELEGANT SQUARE, 1990. Once the home of great art collector Henry McIlhenny, this Rittenhouse Square residence welcomed celebrities like Princess Margaret, Brooke Astor, Tennessee Williams, and Andy Warhol. McIlhenny's collection of art included paintings by Cézanne, Renoir, Degas, Picasso, and Toulouse-Lautrec. Reminiscent of a Parisian park, Rittenhouse Square has long been home to the city's movers and shakers. (PHC.)

AN IMPOSING SYMMETRICAL FAÇADE, *C.* 1960. Green Street was developed from 1860 to 1890, when wealthy industrialists flocked to the area. The street's quality row houses are unlike any in the city. The Kemble-Bergdol Mansion was built in 1890 by William H. Kemble, a city financier, and later sold to the Bergdol family. The Italianate brownstone house's elaborate interior was designed by George Herzog (1851–1920). (PHC.)

SHED FOR ONE AND ALL, C. 1970. The Reading Railroad train shed was designed by the Wilson Brothers in 1891–1893. At its completion, it was the largest single-span structure in the world. It is now the only surviving arched train shed in the country. In Bendiner's Philadelphia, Alfred Bendiner wrote, "Beneath the vast shed remains that amazing market, full of beautiful smells of up-country Dutch goodness, meats, sea food, scrapple and Bassett's ice cream, and family-pride butchers and bakers and sugar-plum manufacturers." (PHC.)

THE BUCK STOPS HERE, C. 1979. A solid, end-of-the-road-style doorway and stairs are seen on this Center City house. (David S. Traub.)

Three

THE MODERN HOUSES AND BEYOND

CITY OF NIGHT, 2002. In this night scene, the Benjamin Franklin Bridge soars over the Delaware River. Designed by French architect Paul P. Cret, the 9, 650-foot-long and 128-foot-wide bridge was opened in 1926 after a seven-year construction period. When built, it became the largest suspension bridge in the world, and for a time it was called the Delaware River Port Authority Bridge. The bridge's computer-driven lighting system is illuminated whenever passing trains trigger sensors. At that point, the cables are lit up in quick succession. (Robert Gordon.)

ANGEL TRIUMPHANT, 2001. Philadelphia's Thirtieth Street Station was designed by Graham, Anderson, Probst, and White and built in 1929 through 1934. The interior ceiling is painted red, gold, and cream. The structure is a good example of a blend between historical and modern styles. When completed, it had a landing strip on the roof for small aircraft. Walter Hancock's angel sculpture commemorates employees of the Pennsylvania Railroad who died in World War II. Cira Centre, a high-rise tower near Thirtieth Street Station was designed by world-renowned architect Cesar Pelli, and was completed in late 2005. (PHC.)

WHERE'S THE PHANTOM?, 1963. This interior view of the Academy of Music shows the huge Victorian chandelier. Here, concert goers prepare for the entrance of conductor Leopold Stokowski. Ulysses S. Grant was nominated for president on the stage of the academy. (Joe Nettis.)

TRADITION DOES NOT MEAN A DEAD TOWN, 1960. The Benjamin Franklin Parkway has been compared to the Champs-Elysees in Paris with its notable Beaux Arts and French classical buildings. In *What I Saw in America*, G. K. Chesterton wrote, "It is at least as possible for a Philadelphian to feel the presence of Penn and Franklin as for an Englishman to see the ghosts of Alfred or Becket. Tradition does not mean a dead town; it does not mean that the living are dead but that the dead are alive. It means that it still matters what Penn did two hundred years ago. . . . I never could feel that in New York that it mattered what anybody did an hour ago." (Joe Nettis.)

SEDATE SPLASH, 1960. The Swann Fountain, situated in Logan Circle on the Benjamin Franklin Parkway, was one of the original park squares laid out by William Penn more than 200 years ago. The fountain was named after William Carey Swann, founder of the Philadelphia Fountain Society, a 19th-century organization dedicated to building drinking fountains for both people and horses. The reclining figures around the fountain symbolize the three main waterways of the city. (Joe Nettis.)

STREETS OF NORTH PHILADELPHIA, 1959. Before 1870, North Philadelphia was a hotbed of horse-racing taverns and farmland. By the late 1890s, however, the city's managerial class began to build new homes here. Later, row houses dotted the landscape, such as these on Dauphin Street and Germantown Avenue. Former North Philadelphia families included Edwin Forrest, prominent in theater, and Peter A. Widener, known for transportation. Today, North Philadelphia is the home of Temple University. (Joe Nettis.)

WHAT A GARGOYLE SEES, 1963. In *Philadelphia Discovered*, Nathaniel Burt stated the following: "Philadelphia is a small city: this is what makes it special. For all the huge body of it, the population and all the statistics of size and worth, it is a very intimate place. Other cities, too, can boost of tonnages and capital and votes delivered. But nobody can call Chicago or New York or Los Angeles or Detroit 'cozy.' Philadelphia is cozy." (Joe Nettis.)

HATCH A BIG EGG, C. 1963. The John Wanamaker building was designed in the Italian Renaissance style by D. H. Burnham and Company and John T. Windrim. Burnham, a Chicago architect, gave the exterior little ornament, the handsome granite and limestone façade evoking a Renaissance palace. The extraordinary interior court raises five floors. John Wanamaker, a South Philadelphia legend, opened his first clothing store at Sixth and Market Streets in 1861, after he was rejected for military service in the Civil War for being "too feeble." (Joe Nettis.)

THE CURTIS INSTITUTE OF MUSIC, 1980. Architects Brack and Douglas Gordon designed the Curtis Institute of Music on Rittenhouse Square in 1897. Once the home of banker George Childs Drexel, the building was used as an all-scholarship music school in 1924 after its founding by Mary Louise Curtis Bok Zimbalist. Famous composers and musicians who taught and studied here include Samuel Barber, Gian Carlo Menotti, Leonard Bernstein, Anna Moffo, and Ned Rorem. (PHC.)

THE BLUE BOOK FAÇADE, 1970. The eight-story Belgravia building (Peale House), with its flamboyantly romantic façade, was one of the first high-rises in the city to use a steel skeletal construction while maintaining traditional design values. Built in 1902 as an apartment house, it was once home to the city's most influential families. The building's architects were Samuel Milligan and Frederich Webber. According to Philadelphia Historical Society records, the Belgravia's elite or blue book recorded a number of prominent guests at weddings and holiday parties from 1904 to 1913, including Emlen and Gloria Etting. (PHC.)

FILM NOIR BACKDROP, 1966. Architect Verus T. Ritter, who had an independent practice in Williamsport before moving to Philadelphia in 1917, formed a partnership with Howell L. Shay in 1920. Ritter and Shay designed commercial and educational buildings, including the U.S. Customs House at Second and Chestnut Streets (pictured), the Francis Drake Hotel, and the Packard Building, at 111 South Fifteenth Street. The firm dissolved in 1936, at which point Ritter became president of the Delaware Tunnel Corporation, an organization that sought to build a tunnel beneath the Delaware River to link South Philadelphia with New Jersey. (PHC.)

STAIRWAY TO SURGERY, *C.* **1945.** Architect Frank V. Nickels received his diploma in architecture from Drexel University in 1914, the same year that he began his independent projects. From 1917 to 1922, Nickels's office was located in the Real Estate Trust Building, and from 1923 to 1935, on South Twenty-first Street. Nazareth Hospital in Northeast Philadelphia was one of his many projects for the Archdiocese of Philadelphia. (Sisters of the Holy Family of Nazareth.)

SOCIETY HILL TOWERS, 2005. Edmund Bacon, city planner from 1948 to 1970 and an architect, sponsored several design competitions for the remake of the city's Delaware River area. Bacon's plan resulted in the I. M. Pei–designed Society Hill Towers, as seen here from Head House Square. A graduate of Cornell University and the Cranbrook Academy of Art, Bacon was awarded the American Institute of Planners Distinguished Service Award for his innovations. (David S. Traub.)

GOING TO THE CHAPEL, C. 1960. The chapel at Nazareth Hospital, pictured here, was designed by Frank V. Nickels. Nickels also designed a huge apartment complex for Philadelphia's African American community. In *Philadelphia: A 300-Year History*, Russell Weigley wrote the following: "The third project, also an apartment complex, was a gift to Philadelphia's black community by Benjamin and Pearl Mason. The Masons had been on relief for five years when they won $150,000 in the Grand National Steeple-chase Sweepstakes in 1940. Shortly thereafter the most heartwarming proposal of all was underway. Having paid the debts owed, the Masons invested some $80,000 of their winnings in building the Frances Plaza Apartments at Nineteenth and Lombard Streets. Twenty-eight tenements were bought around that corner with the aid of Raymond Pace Alexander, a well-known black attorney. Frank V. Nickels, architect, designed a three-story, cream-colored brick apartment house, with court, play space, and gymnasium so arranged that about 40 percent of the land remained open, carrying out Mrs. Mason's wishes as she had expressed them to Alexander." (Sisters of the Holy Family of Nazareth.)

A PIECE OF CHICAGO, C. 1978. Typical of the so-called Chicago commercial style, the 1897 Land Title Building by D. H. Burnham and Company is an excellent example of skyscraper design in early-19th-century Philadelphia. The building's granite, rusticated Ionic arcade and the buffed brick upper stories sets it apart from other high rises on South Broad Street. The Foundation for Architecture has called the building "the earliest east-coast example of this style by a major Chicago architect." (PHC.)

CLASSICAL BEAUX ARTS WITH A TWIST, *C.* 1963. Designed by Horace Trumbauer in the conservative, classical style with Beaux Arts elements, the Widener Building was the last project of P. A. B. Widener, the richest man in Philadelphia at the time of his death in 1915. Built at the cost of nearly $8 million, the structure, with its tri-level plastered façades, steel ornamentation, and steel-framed windows, continues to complement other nearby architectural works such as city hall and the John Wanamaker building. The arcade was closed in 1963 but reopened after Francis Cauffman Foley Hoffmann Architects began restorative work in 1992. (PHC.)

THE DRAKE, C. 1980. The Drake Building, at
Fifteenth and Spruce Streets, looms like a muscular
fortress in downtown Philadelphia. Built in 1929, the
33-story Spanish Baroque, art deco building contains
terra-cotta motifs of dolphins, shells, sailing vessels,
and globes. Its huge terra-cotta dome crowns a steel-
frame structure layered with Pompeian brick. Designed
by architects Ritter and Shay, the upper floors of the
building were influenced by 1920s zoning laws that
required setbacks. (PHC.)

GRAND OLD LADY OF GERMANTOWN, C. 1979. Inspired by British castles of the 13th to 18th centuries, architect Kenneth M. de Vos traveled from England to design Alden Park Manor, a 1,000-unit apartment house on 37 acres perched high over Fairmount Park. Built in the 1920s on the site of the Addison Hutton–designed Justus Strawbridge mansion, this National Register of Historic Places building includes corner capitals from Nottinghameshire, England, and Oriel windows from a 16th-century English church. (PHC.)

ARTISTRY OF IRON, C. 1978. In 1924, the Packard Building was the standard for high-priced rental properties in the city. Architects Ritter and Shay designed the landmark building in 1924; the following year, Shay was awarded a medal from the Philadelphia chapter of the AIA for this Revival-style skyscraper. Today, the building is called the Grande. (PHC.)

BETH SHOLOM SYNAGOGUE, C. 1963. Frank Lloyd Wright's Beth Sholom Synagogue in Elkins Park has been called a spectacular spiritual space, with its sloping floor, translucent pyramidal roof, and colored glass chandelier. Beth Sholom was designed and built in 1959–1960, toward the end of Wright's career. Like many of the buildings of Wright, Beth Shalom's building has flaws. "There are

leaks in the synagogue, but we are surviving," said Gabriel Basch, a Beth Shalom board member. "Over the years we've done a considerable amount of improvement with the structure. It takes about 60 to 70 percent more maintenance on a Wright building."

WILLIAM PENN'S TRADEMARK SHIELD, C. 1990. The Clinical Research Building, School of Medicine, at the University of Pennsylvania, was designed to allow for future changes in equipment and the size of research groups. One of the challenges that Venturi, Scott Brown and Associates, Incorporated faced in designing the building was connecting it both physically and visually to the campus and the medical school. The building was completed in 1990 and bears a huge "icon" of William Penn's trademark shield. (VSBA.)

ON A CLEAR DAY, 2005. The skyscraper boom in Philadelphia continues with the $465 million 57-story Comcast tower (not pictured) at Seventeenth Street and JFK Boulevard, planned for an August 2007 opening. The 975-foot glass tower would be the fifth or sixth tallest building in the country. The design of the new tower has been described as a European-style column of nonreflective glass. Architect Robert A. A. Stern says that the building will be "spectacularly lit at night." As the nation's largest cable television provider, Comcast signed a 15.5-year lease with Liberty Property Trust, the real estate company founded by now-deceased Williard Rouse III, the visionary responsible for breaking Philadelphia's 100-year-old "gentleman's agreement" building height limit. (Joel Kaylor.)

THE MONOLITH AS A WORK OF ART, C. 2001.
Considered by many architecture critics to be one of
the most notable buildings in Philadelphia, Louis Kahn's
Richards Medical Research Laboratory, near the campus
of the University of Pennsylvania, continues to attract
international attention. In his 1960 essay "Form and
Design," Kahn wrote that while visiting the site during the
construction of the frame of the building, he noticed a crane
picking up 25-ton members and swinging them "into places
like matchsticks." He continues, "I resented the garishly
painted crane, this monster which humiliated my building
to be out of scale. I watched the crane go through its many
movements all the time calculating how many more days
this 'thing' was to denominate the site before a flattering
photograph of the building could be made."

Regarded as one of the most important buildings in modern
American architecture, the Richards Medical Research
Laboratory in University City, at Thirty-seventh Street and
Hamilton Walk, was the catapult that brought Louis Kahn's
work to the world stage. Architect Robert Stern calls the
building's internal spaces "majestic in their emptiness" and
notes that the "casually grouped, light, industrial furniture
used in them is not dwarfed." (David S. Traub.)

RESPECTING THE URBAN CONTEXT, 2005. The Kimmel Center for the Performing Arts, at 260 South Broad Street, is Philadelphia's 2,547-seat concert hall. Ground was broken in 1998, and the center, designed by Rafael Vinoly, opened in 2001. Vinoly states, "The tradition of architectural excellence is enormous in Philadelphia. How do you respond to that? You have to make a landmark for a city of monuments, and at the same time you want to invite interaction." (Joel Kaylor.)

PUTTING ON THE RITZ, 2003. *Architecture Digest*'s July 2002 edition reported, "In June 2000 the former Girard Trust complex reopened as the new Ritz-Carlton, Philadelphia. James Garrison, a senior associate of The Hillier Group, a distinguished international firm that specializes in historic preservation, led the elite troops who performed the transformation in an astoundingly brief 18 months." (Hillier Gropu and Tom Crane.)

HIGH OVER RITTENHOUSE SQUARE, C. 2000. The ever-changing skyline of Philadelphia is sometimes threatened with unwise development. A planned 35-story building at Eighteenth and Sansom Streets (not pictured) caused some residents of Rittenhouse Square to organize against the demolition of four historic structures at that corner. Stuart Feldman, a member of SOS, observed, "The site is one of the last two open spaces that give the square and its visitors the sweep of the sky and a feeling of openness and spaciousness in a crowded downtown." (Hillier Group.)

VENTURE IN PHILADELPHIA, 1997. Contrast and analogy describe the Ray and Diana Vagelas Laboratories at the University of Pennsylvania. Winner of the Brick in Architecture Award (AIA), in 1999, the building contributes to the historical setting on the University of Pennsylvania campus and provides a harmonious background for the nearby Furness library. (VSBA.)

A MIGHTY FORTRESS, 1998. Architect David S. Traub poses before one of his projects, the Junod Recreation Center for the city of Philadelphia, on Dunks Ferry Road in Northeast Philadelphia, completed in 1998. (David S. Traub.)

WORLD-FAMOUS PSFS BUILDING, *c.* **1980.** Built in 1930–1932, the PSFS building is considered to be a masterpiece. Architects George Howe and William Lescaze were awarded the gold medal of the AIA's Philadelphia chapter for their design. The PSFS building also received the Building of the Century Award from the same organization. (PHC.)

RITTENHOUSE SQUARE CAFÉ LIFE, 2001. Café life along the square is abundant and reminiscent of some parts of Paris. Because the sidewalks are narrow, café owners who line the sidewalks with two rows of tables instead of one often risk the ire of pedestrians and residents who compare the "two lanes" to an obstacle course. (David S. Traub.)

GOODBYE, GENTLEMAN'S AGREEMENT, 2000. At 960 feet and 61 stories tall, One Liberty Place (L) by Murphy-Jahn and the Zeidler Roberts Partnership, was completed in 1987. Developer Willard Rouse challenged Philadelphia's 100-year-old gentleman's agreement that no building be taller than the 491-foot city hall tower. The great controversy had height-limit traditionalists citing the end of western civilization. Ultimately, money talked, and the project was approved by virtue of the potential increase in revenue and jobs. A combination of silver and blue glass gives the building an illuminated quality. In 1987, Liberty Place ranked 12th among the world's tallest buildings. (David S. Traub.)

BIG DOME GLASS ATRIUM, 2003. One and Two
Liberty Place were built in 1985–1990 with the hope of
"rebirthing" downtown Philadelphia. The Murphy and
Jahn buildings feature a two-level, 90-foot glass shopping
atrium, the nexus for 70 stores, and a food court with 18
restaurants. (David S. Traub.)

THE SHOCK OF THE NEW, *c*. 1960. It has been said that when the PSFS building was built in 1932 that it knocked conservative Philadelphia on its ear. With its red neon rooftop sign (PSFS), and unornamented façade, the building was a design revolution inside and out. Architects George Howe (Philadelphia) and William Lescaze (a Swiss born modernist) designed the furniture, doorknobs, coat hooks, and hinges. In 2004, Yale University's Art and Architecture Gallery celebrated the building with an exhibition entitled, "Nothing More Modern." (PHC.)

SACRED PLACES AND OTHER WORLDS, 2005. In her biography of Frank Lloyd Wright, Ada Louise Huxtable wrote that he "created and embraced his role of independent, nonconforming outsider whose personal search for knowledge and self-realization left conventional learning in the dust." The only major Frank Lloyd Wright building in the Philadelphia area, Beth Sholom Synagogue, with its translucent pyramidal roof, inwardly sloping floor, and hexagonal plan, is a masterpiece of religious architecture. The synagogue can hold 1,000 people and was a conceptional project of Wright's for years before its materialization on the architect's drafting board. (Joel Kaylor.)

ONE LOGAN SQUARE, 2005. This 30-story office tower on Logan Square hides the lower eight-story, 450-room Four Seasons Hotel. The buildings, which were completed in 1983, won the New York State Award for Design Excellence. (Joel Kaylor.)

THE HILLIER GROUP'S GRAND HOTEL, 2003. "The Ritz-Carlton in Philadelphia is an authentically grand hotel. It opened only two years ago, but its history, architectural and social, has the patina of an old portrait—perhaps one of Sargent's pensive heiresses, pale as cameo, whose aura of serene gentility belies a romantic past," reported *Architectural Digest* in 2002. (Hillier Group and Tom Crane.)

SHOP AT BEST BUY, THE GREAT NORTHEAST, 1998. Modern shopping mall–style architecture can be appreciated for its easy charms. (David S. Traub.)

SCALING THE BELL ATLANTIC BUILDING, 2005. The striking 55-story Bell Atlantic Building, with its flat roof and warm red color, was designed by Philadelphia's Kling Lindquist Partnership. The building opened in 1991. Architecture critic Paul Goldeberger compared the building to New York's 30 Rockefeller Plaza, calling it "a firm stable presence on the skyline with enough rhythm to its shape to keep the eye engaged." In addition, the AIA deemed the building "the best of a recent crop of towers." (Joel Kaylor.)

THE SKYSCRAPER WITHIN, 2001. While the Venturi-Brown imprint can be found on buildings all over the world, it is true that there are startingly few Venturi buildings in Philadelphia. The Anna Venturi house in Chestnut Hill (pictured), the renovated Irvine Auditorium at the University of Pennsylvania, Franklin Court in Old City, the Clinical Research building, and the Roy and Diana Vagelos Labs at Penn are some notable exceptions.

"With Guild House and the Vanna Venturi house, the Venturi firm had found its voice. The powerful synthesis of new visual and new social thinking became the foundation for all their subsequent activities," wrote Brownplee, De Long, and Hiesinger in *Out of the Ordinary*, a 2001 study of the architects' work. (VSBA and Rollin La France.)

UNITING PAST AND PRESENT, 1970. An elegant Corinthian column rises in the Great Court of Pennsylvania Hospital. Designed to be the residences of officers and servants in the late 1700s, the Great Court also houses the original apothecary and historic library. Fro the 1976 Bicentennial, the court was painted white, a traditional colonial color. (PHC.)

WILLIAM PENN'S CONSTANTINOPLE, 1967. Designed to resemble the Hagia Sofia (St. Sophia) Cathedral in Constantinople (now Istanbul), the Ukrainian Catholic Cathedral in Northern Liberties is 172 feet long, 128 feet wide, and 106 feet high. The interior of the cathedral's dome is layered with quarter-inch-square Venetian glass tiles composed of 22-karat gold fused in glass. (PHC.)

GRAVES ON BROAD STREET, 2005. World-renowned architect Michael Graves added this vertical addition to a Center City parking garage on Philadelphia's Avenue of the Arts (Broad Street) in the late 1980s. Graves, born in Indianapolis, Indiana, in 1934, studied at the University of Cincinnati and Harvard. He became one of the world's preeminent post-modern architects in the 1980s with his transformation of the rational style of Le Corbusier into a neoclassical one in which columns, pediments, and arches are used to create buildings with whimsy and sophistication. The so-called Graves Style also celebrates architectural pastiche and kitsch. (David S. Traub.)

MAN OF LETTERS, 2005. The author, Thom Nickels, stands before the Man of Letters' Letter Box in Philadelphia's historic Bellevue Stratford building. (David S. Traub.)